Grade Eight

Acoustic Guitar Playing

Compiled and edited by
Tony Skinner and Laurence Harwood for

RGT®
Registry of Guitar Tutors

A CIP record for this publication is available from the British Library
ISBN: 978-1-905908-08-0

Printed and bound in Great Britain

Published by Registry Publications

REGISTRY PUBLICATIONS LTD

Registry Mews, 11-13 Wilton Rd, Bexhill, Sussex, TN40 1HY

Compiled by

RGT®

Registry of Guitar Tutors

Acknowledgements
The editors are grateful for the advice and support of all members of the RGT's Acoustic Guitar Advisory Panel during the compilation of this series. Thanks are due to Al Summers for his input to the Aural Assessments, and to Stuart Ryan for his work on the CD.

Cover design and photography by JAK Images; back cover photographs courtesy of Moon Guitars and Freshman Guitars.

CONTENTS

CD LISTING

INTRODUCTION

This publication is part of a progressive series of ten handbooks, primarily intended for candidates considering taking a Registry Of Guitar Tutors (RGT) examination in acoustic guitar playing. However, given each handbook's wide content of musical repertoire and associated educational material, the series provides a solid foundation of musical education for any acoustic guitar student – whether intending to take an examination or not.

Those preparing for an examination should use this handbook in conjunction with the Acoustic Guitar Exam Information Booklet and Acoustic Guitar Syllabus – both freely downloadable from the RGT website: www.RegistryOfGuitarTutors.com

CD

A CD is supplied with this handbook as a learning aid and the recorded performances are designed specifically to provide an indication of the standard of playing expected at this grade.

FINGERING OPTIONS

The fingerings (including tablature positions) that have been used in this handbook are those that are most likely to be effective for the widest range of players at this level. However, there is a variety of alternative fingerings that could be used, and any systematic and effective fingerings that produce a good musical result will be acceptable; there is no requirement to use the exact fingerings shown within this handbook. Throughout the examination, it is entirely the candidate's choice as to whether a pick (plectrum) or fingers are used to pick the strings. A thumbpick can be used if desired.

TUNING

The use of an electronic tuner or other tuning aid, prior to or at the start of the examination, is permitted; candidates should be able to make any further adjustments, if required during the examination, unaided. The examiner will, upon request, offer an E or A note to tune to.

For examination purposes guitars should be tuned to Standard Concert Pitch (A=440Hz). A tuning guide is provided on the accompanying CD on Track 1.

EXAMINATION ENTRY

An examination entry form is provided at the back of this handbook. This is the only valid entry form for the RGT acoustic guitar examinations.

Please note that *if the entry form is detached and lost, it will not be replaced under any circumstances* and the candidate will be required to obtain a replacement handbook to obtain another entry form.

The entry form includes a unique entry code to enable you to enter online via the RGT website **www.RegistryOfGuitarTutors.com**

FINGERBOARD KNOWLEDGE

The examiner will choose a selection of the chords, scales and arpeggios listed in this chapter and ask the candidate to play them *from memory*. Candidates can use fingers or a pick (plectrum). The examiner will be listening for accurate, clear, fluent and even playing. Prompt presentations, without undue delay or hesitation, will be taken as an indication of secure knowledge.

A maximum of 10 marks may be awarded in this section of the examination.

CHORDS

At this grade, candidates should be able to play:

- **major chords, with any root note, in four different fingerboard positions.**
- **minor chords, with any root note, in three different fingerboard positions.**
- **the following minor chords in 1st and 2nd inversion: Am, Dm and Em.**

Chords should be played using a single slow strum, starting with the lowest note. The whole chord shape should be carefully placed on the fingerboard before, and kept on during, playing. A string which should not be sounded when playing a chord is marked with an **X** by the fretbox.

In this handbook, transpositional chord shapes that can be moved up or down the fingerboard are used for the multi-position chords. The table below lists the fret position needed to produce chords at different pitches.

First finger on fret number	1	2	3	4	5	6	7	8	9	10	11	12
Chords with root on E string	F	F♯/G♭	G	G♯/A♭	A	A♯/B♭	B	C	C♯/D♭	D	D♯/E♭	E
Chords with root on A string	A♯/B♭	B	C	C♯/D♭	D	D♯/E♭	E	F	F♯/G♭	G	G♯/A♭	A
Chords with root on D string	D♯/E♭	E	F	F♯/G♭	G	G♯/A♭	A	A♯/B♭	B	C	C♯/D♭	D

Major chords in 4 different fingerboard positions

All the chord shapes below are transpositional and can be moved along the fingerboard to another pitch without the need to change fingering. The chord shapes candidates will need to use will depend upon the pitch requested by the examiner.

Below are five transpositional chord shapes illustrated in F major. Candidates should be able to decide which four of these shapes are in accessible fingerboard positions for the pitch requested; an open position chord (or other alternative chord shape) can be used in place of one of the transpositional shapes when appropriate.

F

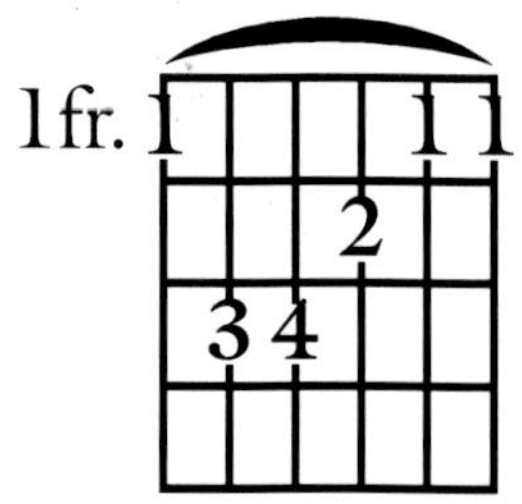

F (root on E string)

F

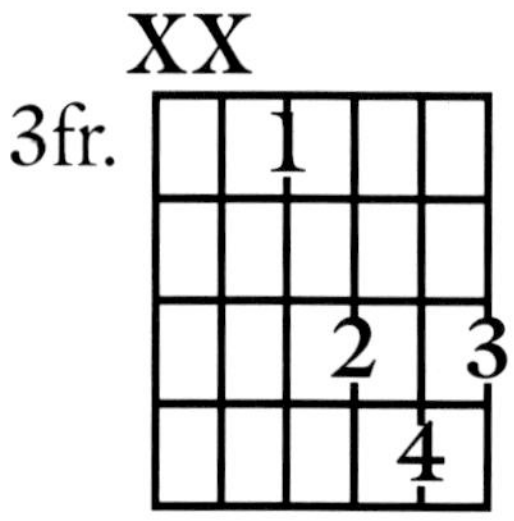

F (root on D string)

F

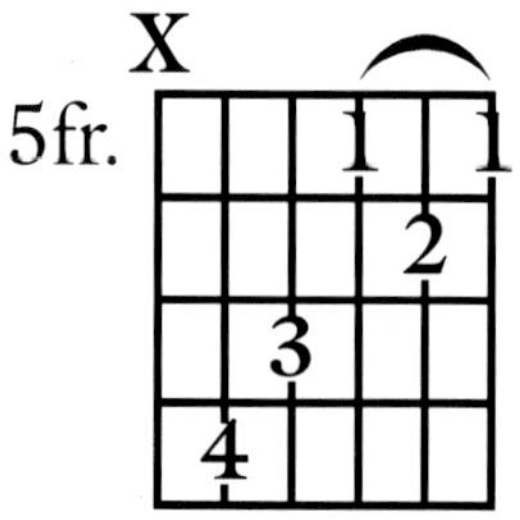

F (root on A string)

F

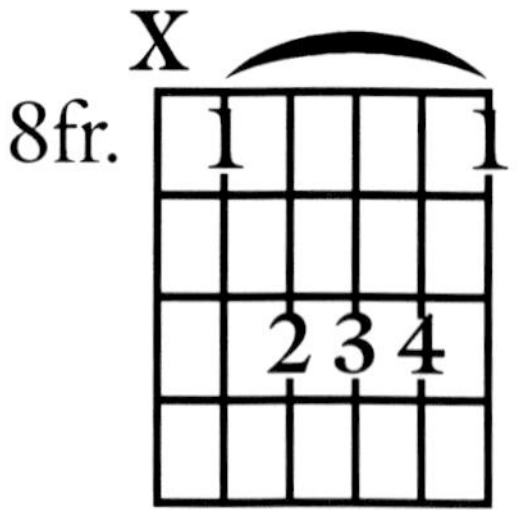

F (root on A string)

F

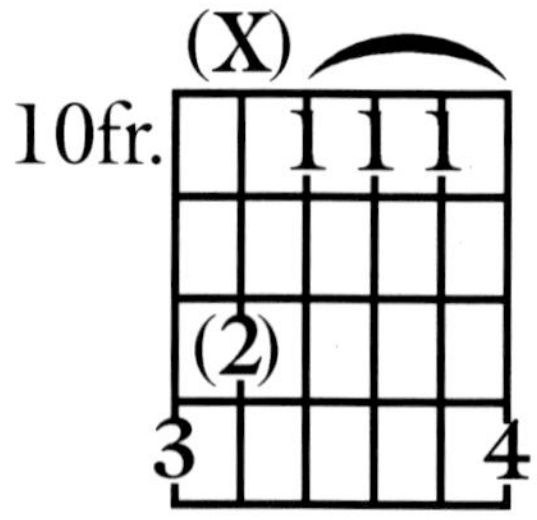

F (root on E string)

For ease of playing and clarity, it is common practice to mute the 5th string when playing this chord shape. Either version will be acceptable in the examination.

Minor chords in 3 different fretboard positions

All the chord shapes illustrated are transpositional and can be moved along the fingerboard to another pitch without the need to change fingering. If preferred, an open position chord can be used in place of one of the transpositional shapes to facilitate playing all three chords in accessible fingerboard positions. The chord shapes you will need to use will depend upon the pitch requested by the examiner. Examples are illustrated overleaf in F minor and B♭ minor, all using transpositional shapes.

Fm

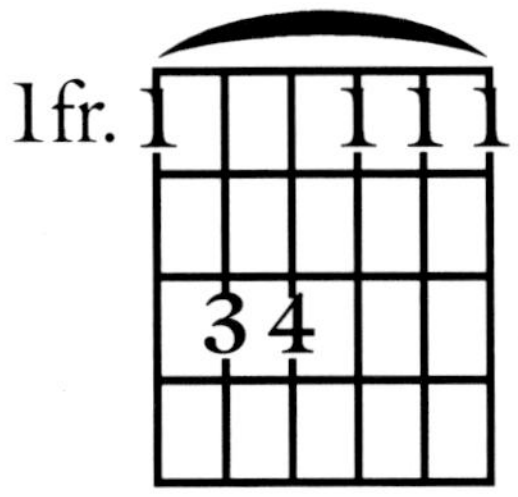

F minor (root on E string)

Fm

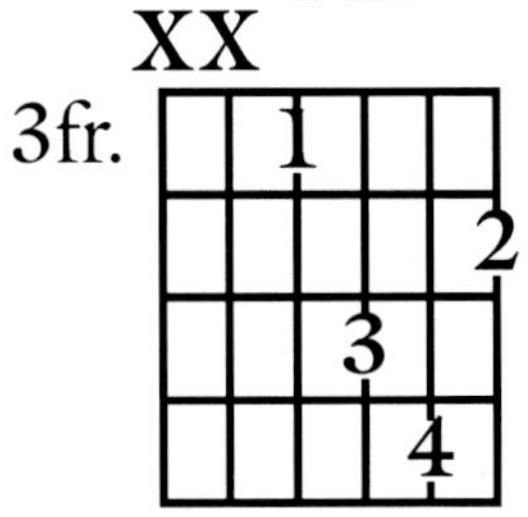

F minor (root on D string)

Fm

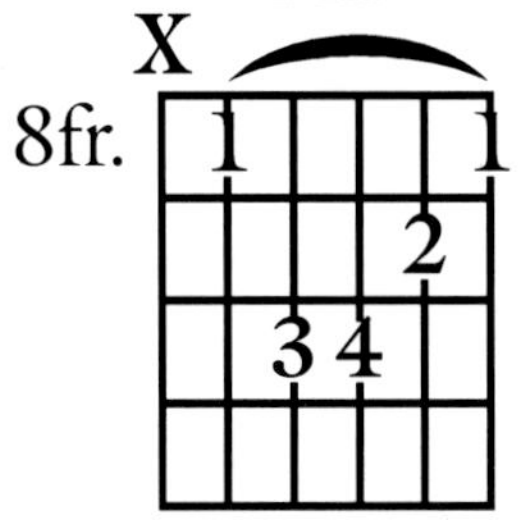

F minor (root on A string)

B♭m

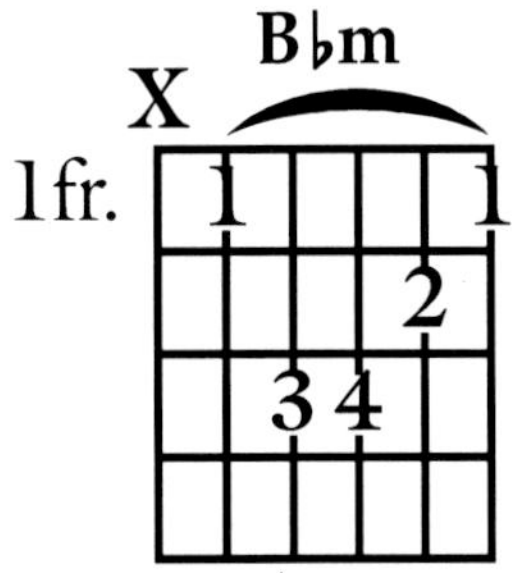

B♭ minor (root on A string)

B♭m

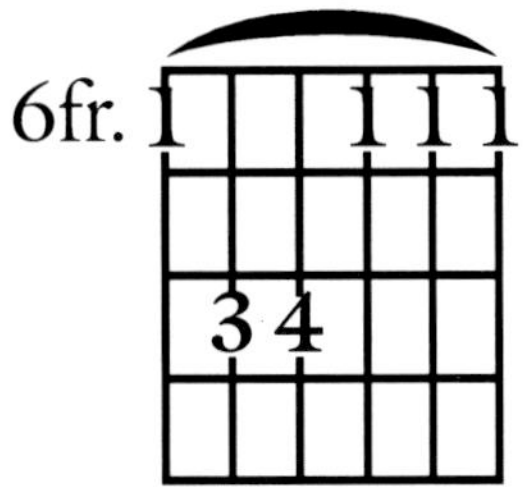

B♭ minor (root on E string)

B♭m

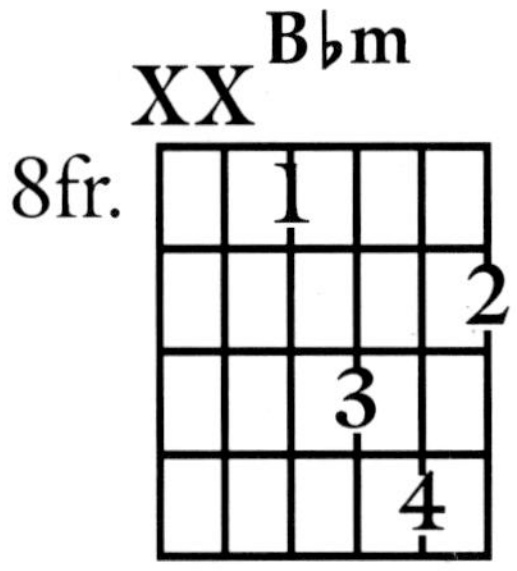

B♭ minor (root on D string)

Minor chords in 1st and 2nd inversions

An inversion occurs when a chord is re-fingered so that one of the notes other than the root note becomes the lowest note. 1st inversion is when the major third of the chord becomes the bass note, 2nd inversion is when the fifth becomes the bass note. Inversions are also commonly referred to as 'slash' chords because of the way the chord symbols are written.

Am/C

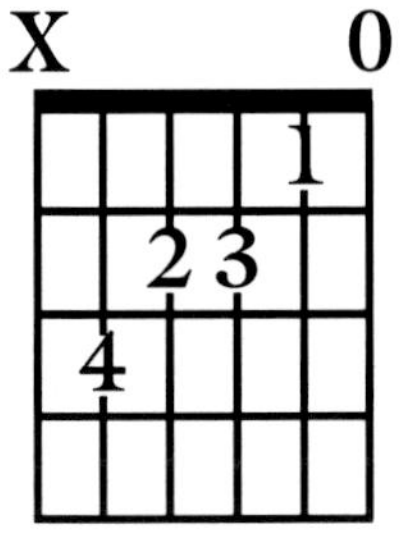

A minor (1st Inversion)

Am/E

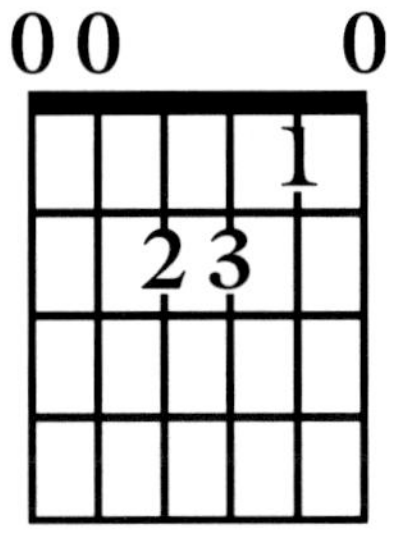

A minor (2nd Inversion)

Dm/F

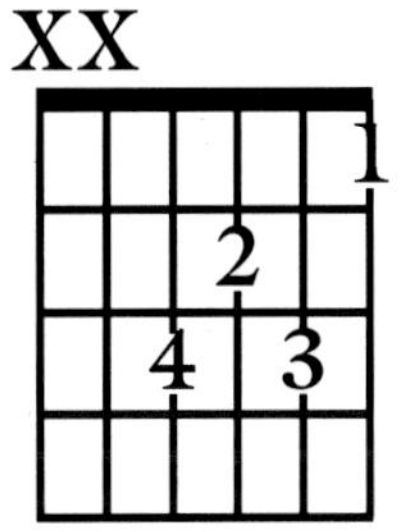

D minor (1st Inversion)

Dm/A

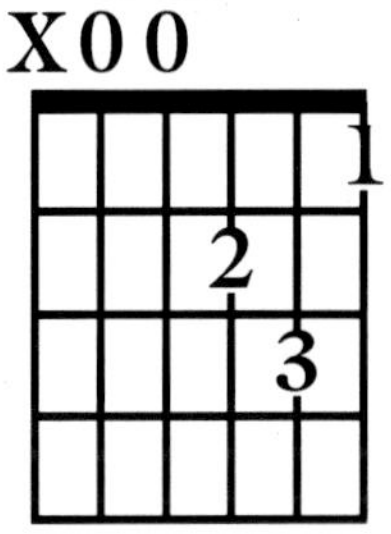

D minor (2nd Inversion)

Em/G

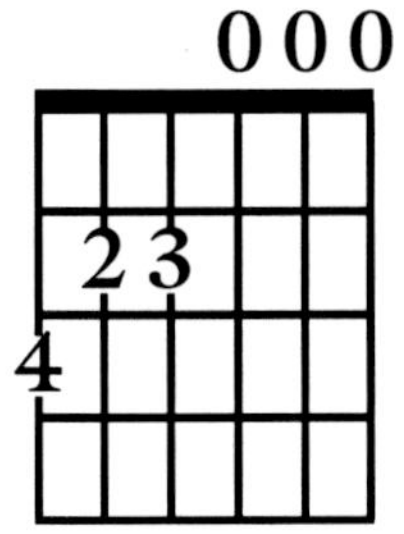

E minor (1st Inversion)

Em/B

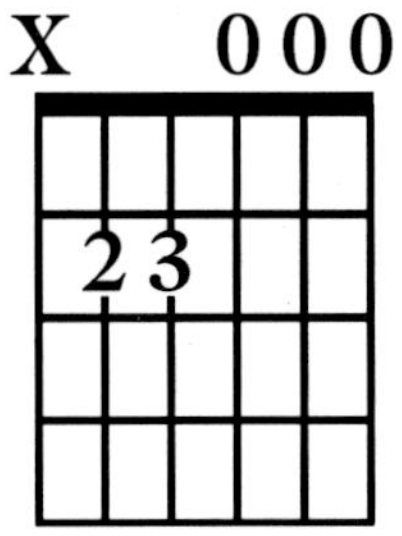

E minor (2nd Inversion)

Candidates are free to use alternative fingerings and different fingerboard positions to the examples illustrated in this handbook.

SCALES

The requirements for Grade Eight are:

- **One octave major scale in five fingerboard positions in *any* accessible key**
- **One octave C major scale harmonised in 3rds**
- **One octave C major scale harmonised in 6ths**
- **One octave G major scale harmonised in 10ths**

One octave major scale shapes are shown with starting notes of both A and E in five fingerboard positions. Candidates should be able to select the shapes best suited to the key they are asked to play in; these may be any combination of the illustrated scale shapes (or other suitable shapes, including open position), providing they are all played at the same octave. Candidates will not be asked to play in keys that would necessitate fingerboard positions that are inaccessible for their particular instrument.

Scales should be played ascending and descending, i.e. from the lowest note to the highest and back again without repeating, or pausing at, the top note. Non-harmonised scales should be played at an *approximate* tempo of 160 beats per minute, with two notes being played for each beat. Harmonised scales should be played at an *approximate* tempo of 66 beats per minute, with two notes being played for each beat.

1 octave A major scale – 5 fingerboard positions

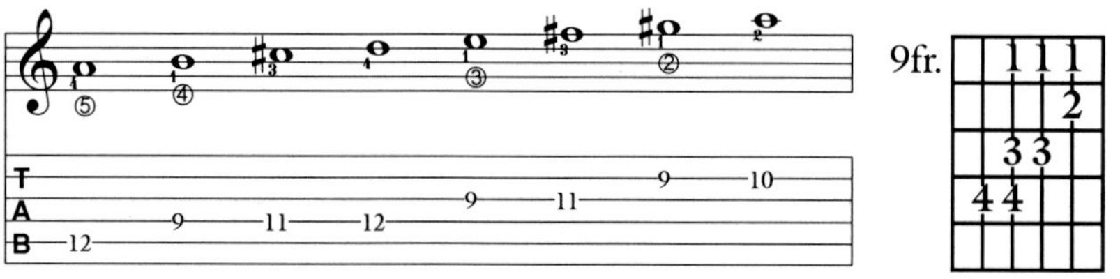

1 octave E major scale – 5 fingerboard positions

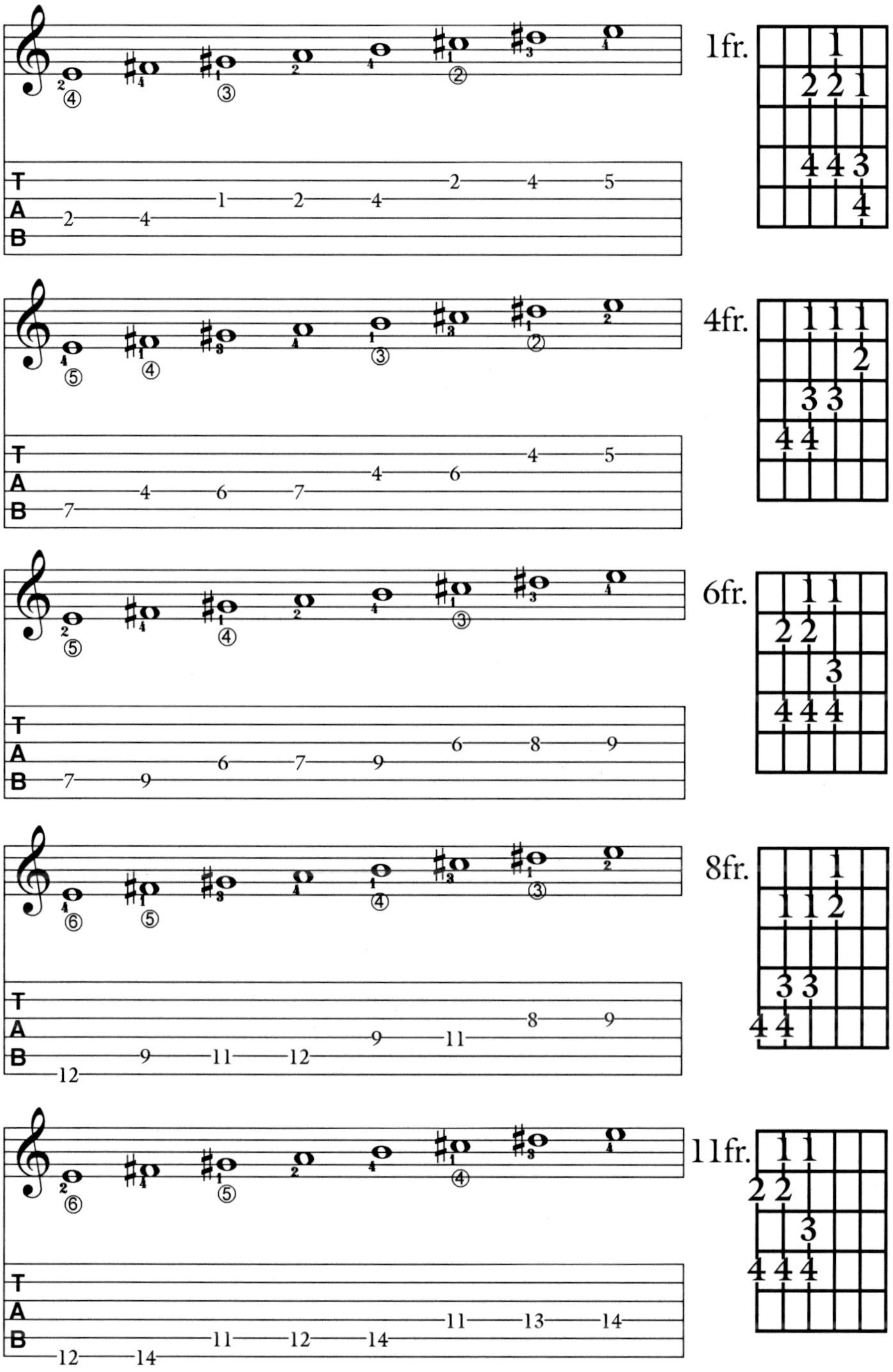

C major harmonised in 3rds – 1 octave

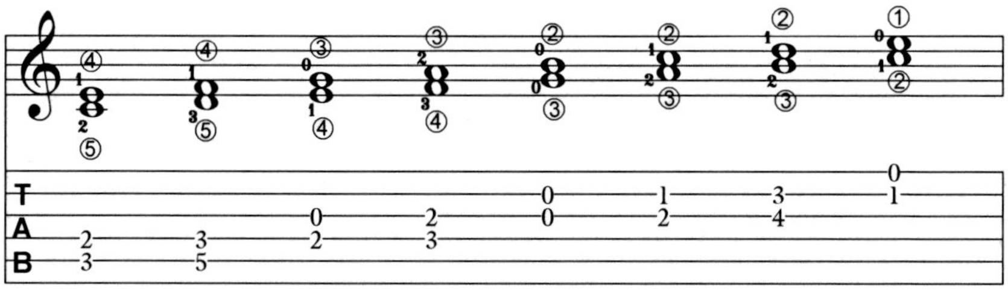

C major harmonised in 6ths – 1 octave

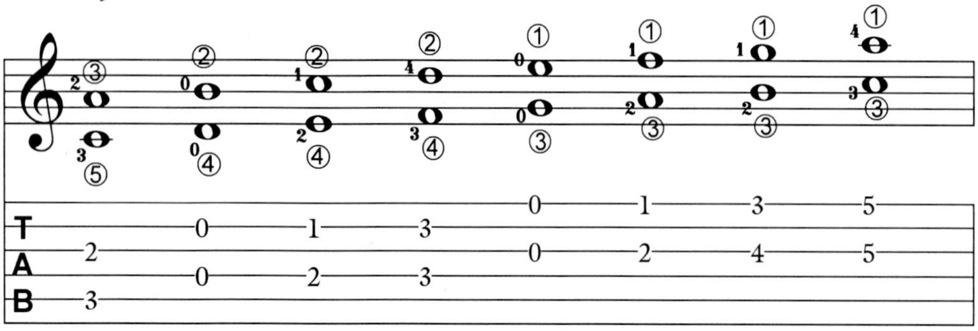

G major harmonised in 10ths – 1 octave

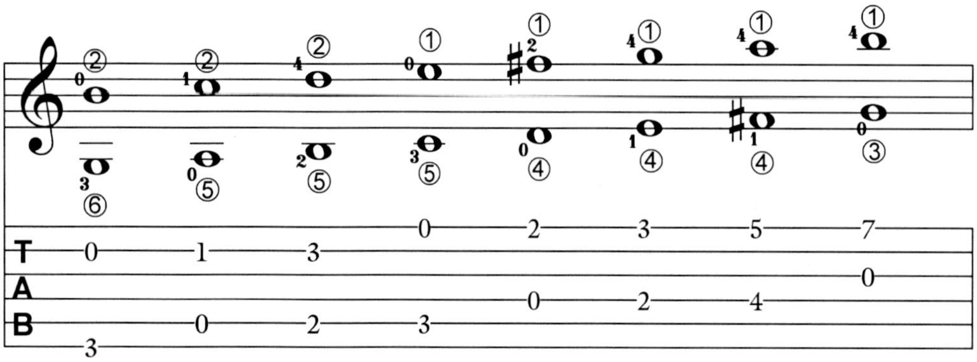

ARPEGGIOS

At this grade candidates should be able to play a two octave dominant seventh arpeggio at any pitch.

The arpeggio is illustrated below with a root note of A and is notated with a transpositional finger pattern, so the shape can be moved up or down the fingerboard to a new pitch without the need for a change of fingering. Candidates will not be asked to play at pitches that would necessitate fingerboard positions that are inaccessible for their particular instrument.

Arpeggios should be played ascending and descending, i.e. from the lowest note to the highest and back again without repeating, or pausing at, the top note. Arpeggios should be played at an approximate tempo of 120 beats per minute, with two notes being played for each beat.

A dominant seventh arpeggio – 2 octaves

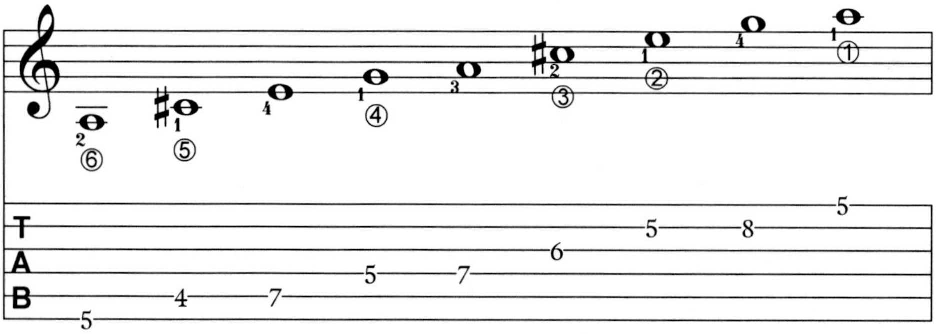

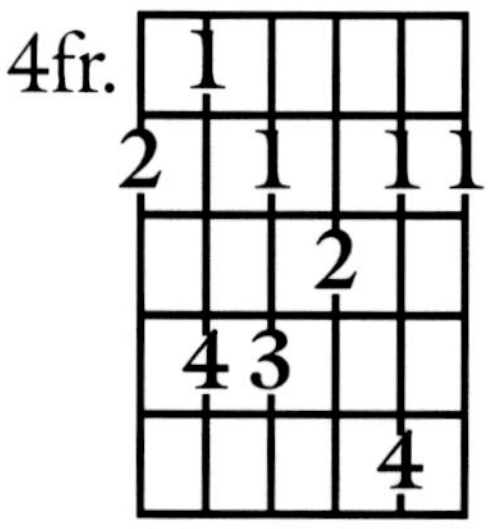

PERFORMANCE

Candidates should perform a total of TWO pieces, demonstrating some variety in musical style and a range of technical ability. At least ONE of the pieces should be chosen from the four notated in this handbook (see pages 13-26). However, instead of playing a second piece from this handbook, candidates can, if they prefer, select *either*:

- ONE piece chosen from the 'List of suggested alternative pieces' for the grade (listed on the RGT website – www.RegistryOfGuitarTutors.com) ***or***
- ONE 'free choice' piece (self-composed or otherwise) providing it is of at least similar standard.

Wherever possible, candidates should bring the notation of any free choice pieces, in standard notation or tablature, to the exam for the examiner to view. Although not mandatory, the free choice may be a piece using altered tuning or specialist styles of guitar playing such as slide guitar.

Candidates are allowed to interpret all solo pieces in their own style, rather than sticking rigidly to the arrangement shown in the notation, providing that the technical level is not simplified.

A maximum of 50 marks may be awarded in this section – each piece has a maximum of 25 marks.

In order to obtain a high mark in the exam, the performances should demonstrate a high level of technical accomplishment, with an appropriate level of accuracy, fluency, clarity, articulation and dynamic range. The degree of musicality will be equally important and the playing should demonstrate a mature sense of musical style with an ability to take charge of expressive elements in the music. The performances should be confident and assured, and should communicate a sense of individual interpretative skill, with a clear ability to engage the listener fully in the performance.

- Tempo markings have been chosen that reflect the capabilities expected at this level, but are for general guidance only: faster, or slightly slower, tempos can be used providing they produce an effective musical result.
- There is a variety of finger positions that could be used and any systematic and effective fingerings that produce a good musical result will be acceptable.
- The CD recordings are provided purely as aural guides to the pieces and are therefore performed with only minimal interpretation; candidates are encouraged to develop their own interpretation of the pieces.

PERFORMANCE NOTES

The Coast Road

This 2004 piece is by the British acoustic guitarist Stuart Ryan and is an arrangement of the title track of his album *The Coast Road*. It is notated here in the key of E major. The piece is in three distinct sections: the opening reflective section in $\frac{4}{4}$ up to bar 15, followed by a slightly faster section in $\frac{3}{4}$ up to bar 40, which is followed by a much faster reel-like second section in $\frac{4}{4}$. Hammer-ons and pull-offs are used in many places to aid fluency. The first two sections can be performed with plenty of rubato to capture the feel of the music (the CD recording is deliberately performed 'straight' to encourage individual interpretation).

Acoustic Fuel

This rock-influenced piece is from British guitarist Chaz Hart's 2001 *Hartbeat* album. It uses a dropped D tuning (i.e. the 6th string is tuned a wholetone down to D). The low bass string is then played repeatedly to create a pedal-tone effect against which the higher notes or chords move to create harmonic variety. The piece relies on the use of dynamic variety to help generate a sense of excitement.

I Dare You

This 2007 piece by guitar educator Tony Skinner has been composed to encourage students to develop fluency in 'rolling' fingerpicking – i.e. picking across the strings in a fast arppegiated style (e.g. in bars 8 and 12, and particularly in bars 28-32). The piece uses DADGAD tuning (the 6th, 2nd and 1st strings are tuned down a wholetone) which allows chords with many open strings to be used and thereby facilitates the use of the fast rolling technique. The piece has been recorded on the accompanying CD at the minimum tempo expected for the grade, but candidates should feel free to attempt it as fast as they dare!

The Derry Hornpipe

This is a traditional Irish hornpipe, arranged here as a flatpicking piece designed to be played with a plectrum. In line with common practice for this genre, the melody has been notated in 'straight eights' for ease of reading, but it is expected that the reader will adapt and interpret the rhythm in the style of a traditional Irish hornpipe – i.e. with a jaunty rhythm somewhere between 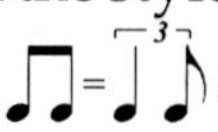 and .

The CD recording provides an example of how this can be played, but any appropriate rhythmic interpretation will be acceptable in the exam. Although the music is notated in $\frac{4}{4}$ time, there should be a strong feel of two-per-bar to capture the natural pulse of this style.

The Coast Road (Stuart Ryan)

11
♩ = 112
15
H P
H P H
19
H P
S
23
H P
H P H

27
H
T
A
B
31
35
1.
2.
♩ = 132
40
P
H
S

Track 2

The Coast Road can be heard on CD track 2

Acoustic Fuel (Chaz Hart)

ff
Count 4's out loud
try playing without bass
p
sim.
H P
H P
H P

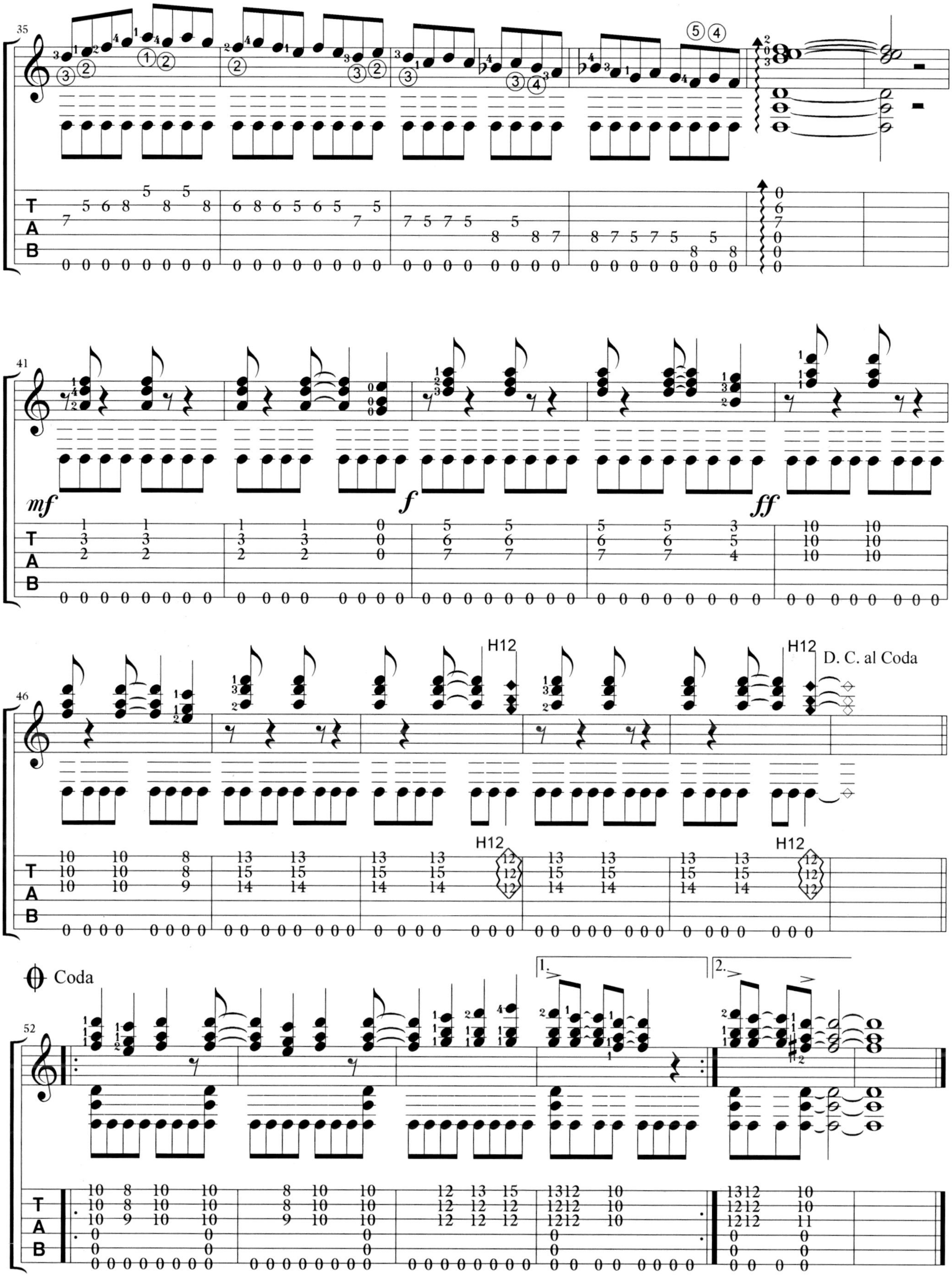

Track 3

Acoustic Fuel can be heard on CD track 3

I Dare You (Tony Skinner)

13
H P
H
H P
H P
D A G D A D
T A B
16
H7
19
21
H P
H
H P
H P

24
H7
H P
D A G D A D
TAB
26
H P
D A G D A D
TAB
28
D A G D A D
TAB
30
D A G D A D
TAB

Track 4 I Dare You can be heard on CD track 4

The Derry Hornpipe (Traditional)

Play with a jaunty hornpipe rhythm (somewhere between ♫ = ♩♪ (triplet) and ♫ = ♪. ♬)

17
TAB
21
TAB
25
TAB
29
TAB
H
P

Track 5 The Derry Hornpipe can be heard on CD track 5

MUSICAL KNOWLEDGE

This section of the exam consists of a discussion between the examiner and the candidate, allowing the candidate an opportunity to display their broad knowledge of acoustic guitar playing.

The primary focus of the discussion will be on the pieces played in the 'Performance' section of the exam, but may extend to wider related topics. The examiner may ask about matters such as:

- the candidate's reasons for choosing the pieces that were performed in the exam
- basic background information about the pieces (period, composer) and the wider acoustic guitar repertoire
- the styles of the pieces performed and how they contrast with other styles and pieces
- the candidate's approach to interpreting the pieces performed
- the content of the pieces performed, including any harmonic, rhythmic or melodic features, the key and time signature, any repeat signs, dynamic markings or other signs that appear in the music
- the technical and musical challenges involved in performing the pieces, including any problems that were encountered when preparing the pieces and how these were overcome
- a critical self-evaluation of the candidate's performance, including aspects which went well and an awareness of aspects which could have been improved
- knowledge of use of the capo and transposition
- knowledge of common altered tunings

The candidate is expected to undertake sufficient research in order to be fully prepared to discuss any of the topics listed above. The examiner will be looking for evidence of careful preparation and a thorough understanding of the repertoire performed, as well as a widening musical and stylistic awareness.

A maximum of ten marks may be awarded in this section of the examination.

In order to gain the highest marks, responses in the discussion should be authoritative, knowledgeable, and well-communicated, employing appropriate musical and technical terminology when necessary.

ACCOMPANIMENT

In this section of the exam, the candidate should play a chordal accompaniment while the examiner plays an eight-bar melody (either live on guitar or keyboard, or via a recording).

- The candidate will be shown a chord chart for the melody. The examiner will then give a one bar count-in and play the melody once for the candidate to listen to without playing along.
- The examiner will then give another one bar count-in and the melody will be played a further three times without stopping. The candidate can accompany the first of these three verses if they wish to, but only the accompaniment of the second and third verses will be assessed.

The range of chords will be restricted to the chords required for this and previous grades. Candidates who are unsure of the chords set for previous grades should refer to the earlier handbooks in this series.

Some bars will be 'split bars' containing two chords. Diagonal lines are used to indicate the division of the bar: the chord symbol representing one beat and each diagonal line representing another beat.

The final chord (after the repeat) should be played with a single strum.

The time signature will be either $\frac{3}{4}$, $\frac{4}{4}$, or $\frac{6}{8}$.

The style of the accompaniment is left to the candidate's discretion, and the candidate can chose to either strum or fingerpick. The CD recording that comes with this book provides an indication of the technical level that would be expected at this grade – only the two assessed verses are provided for each example. It is NOT intended that candidates copy the style of accompaniments performed on the CD recording – these are provided purely as examples of the standard required – and candidates are strongly encouraged to devise their own rhythmic/picking styles; these should always relate to the style and timing of the melody played by the examiner.

The melody notation played by the examiner will not be seen by the candidate.

ACCOMPANIMENT ADVICE

A maximum of 20 marks may be awarded in this section of the exam.

In order to achieve the most musical performance and obtain a high mark in the exam you should aim for the following when performing your accompaniment:

- Remember that the very first time the examiner plays the melody, you have the chance to listen to it without needing to play along. Use this opportunity to listen carefully and try to absorb the style, melodic shape and structure of the melody.
- In the first verse of the three continuous playings your playing will not be assessed, so you can best use this time by reading through the chord chart and just strumming once each chord so that the timing becomes clearly fixed in your mind.
- In the remaining two verses use an appropriate rhythm or picking style that suits the mood, style and timing of the melody.
- The performance should be confident and assured, and should demonstrate a high level of technical ability.
- Keep listening to the melody while playing your accompaniment and make sure to keep in time with it. Change smoothly from one chord to another, whilst making sure your chords ring clear and avoiding excessive fingerboard movement.
- Demonstrate evidence of your musicality by including some appropriate variations. Be creative in your approach and demonstrate expressiveness, and a mature sense of musical style.

Three examples of the *type* of test that will occur are given on the following pages. Note that each of the Accompaniment Examples is provided only as a sample of the *type* of melody and chord symbols that may occur in the exam.

Accompaniment Example 1 (CD track 6)

Chord chart

| 4/4 ||: B♭ / Gm / | Cm | E♭ / F / | B♭ |

| Dm / E♭ F | Cm | E♭ / F Cm | B♭ :|| B♭ ||

Melody

Accompaniment Example 2 (CD track 7)

Chord chart

| 6/8 ‖: G / / G/B / / | Am/C / / Am / / | D / / D/A / / |

| Em/B / / Em / / | C / / C/G / / | Am / / Am/E / / |

| D / / D/F♯ / / | G / / D7 / / :‖ G ‖

Melody

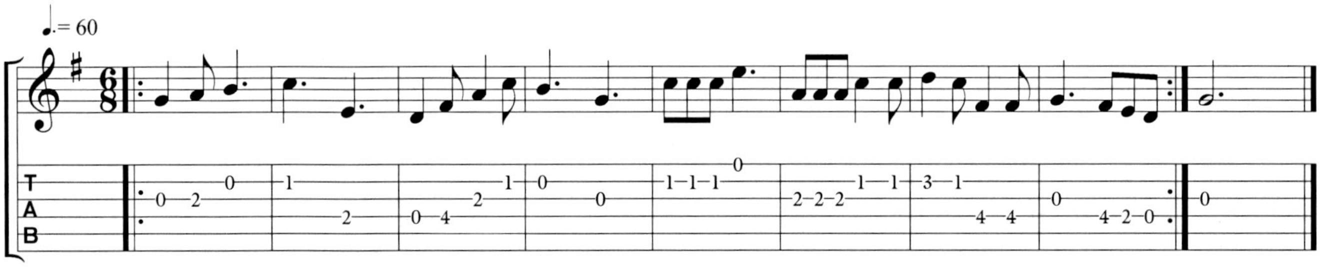

Accompaniment Example 3 (CD track 8)

Chord chart

| 3/4 ‖: A | F♯m7 | Bm7 | E |

| D E D | C♯m | Bm C♯m D | E7 :‖ A ‖

Melody

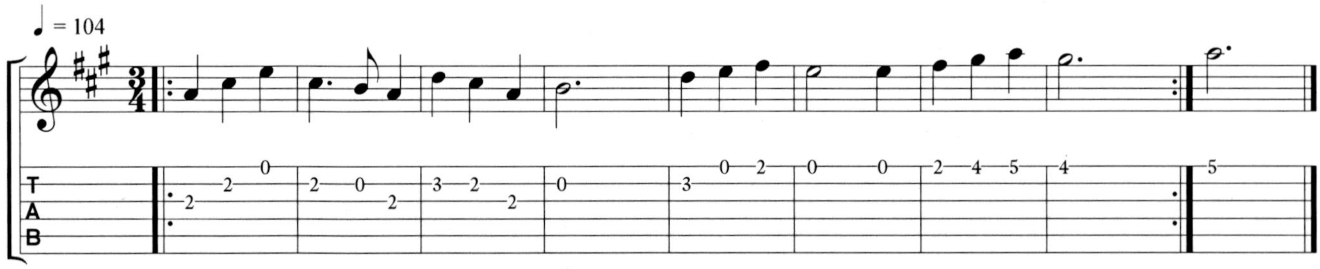

Tracks 6, 7 & 8

Accompaniment Examples 1, 2 & 3 can be heard on CD tracks 6, 7 & 8

AURAL ASSESSMENT

The candidate will be given a selection of rhythm, pitch and harmony tests. The examiner will play these either on guitar or keyboard (live or via a recording). Examples of the tests are provided below; these are also provided on the accompanying CD. A maximum of 10 marks may be awarded in total during this section of the examination.

RHYTHM TESTS

Test A – Keeping time

The examiner will twice play a 4-bar melody in $\frac{2}{4}$, $\frac{3}{4}$, $\frac{4}{4}$, $\frac{6}{8}$ or $\frac{12}{8}$ time. During the second playing the candidate should clap or tap the main pulse (this means 2 beats for $\frac{6}{8}$; 4 beats for $\frac{12}{8}$), accenting the first beat of each bar. The note values will not be shorter than sixteenth notes (semiquavers) and may include dotted notes, triplets, ties and syncopation. The melody may start with one or more pick-up notes. The final bar will be a full bar.

Below is an example of the *style* of test in each of the time signatures, with the correct pulse that the candidate should clap shown between the treble clef and the tablature notation.

Test B – Recognising the time signature

The candidate should identify, without a further hearing, the time signature of the melody from Test A by naming it as $\frac{2}{4}$, $\frac{3}{4}$, $\frac{4}{4}$, $\frac{6}{8}$ or $\frac{12}{8}$.

Test C – Repeating a rhythm

The examiner will play an extract from Test A twice, as marked in the examples. The candidate should reproduce the exact *rhythm* (not just the pulse) by clapping or tapping.

Example 1 (CD track 9)

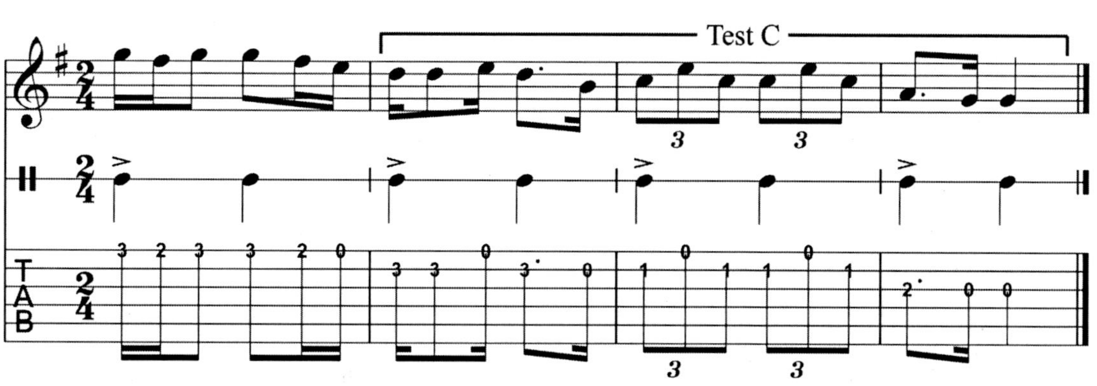

Example 2 (CD track 10)

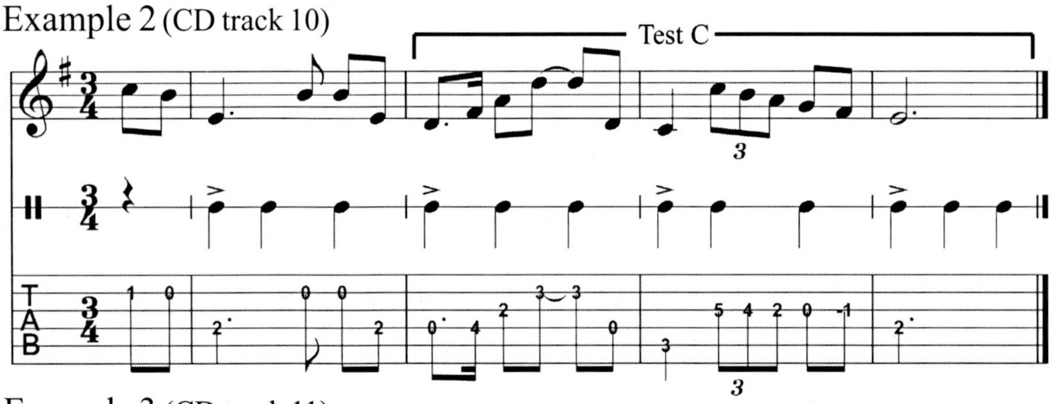

Example 3 (CD track 11)

Example 4 (CD track 12)

Example 5 (CD track 13)

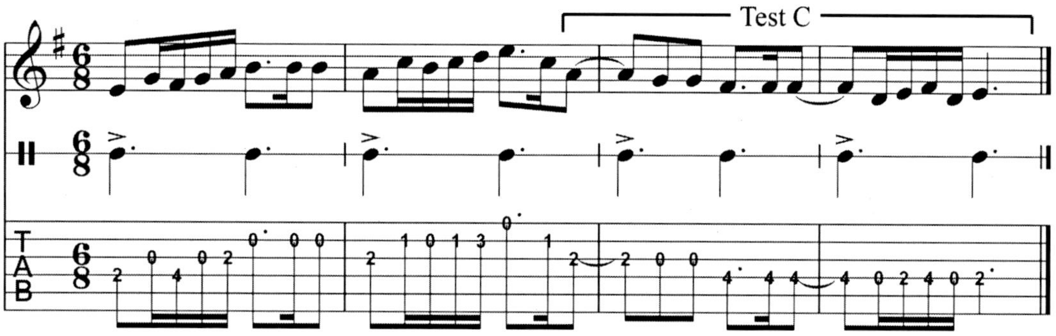

PITCH AND HARMONY TESTS

Test D – Reproducing a phrase

The candidate will be asked to look away while the examiner twice plays a four-bar phrase in $\frac{3}{4}$, $\frac{4}{4}$ or $\frac{6}{8}$ time taken from a major scale in any key. Bars 1 and 3 will be identical. The examiner will name the scale and play the tonic (key) note. The phrase may begin on a keynote or on the third or fifth degree of the scale. The candidate should replicate the phrase on the guitar. If required, the candidate may request to hear the phrase once more but will then be expected to reproduce the phrase promptly with no further attempts.

Time values will be limited to quarter notes (crotchets), dotted quarter notes (dotted crotchets) and eighth notes (quavers).

Below are two examples of the style of test:

Example 1 from C major scale (CD track 14)

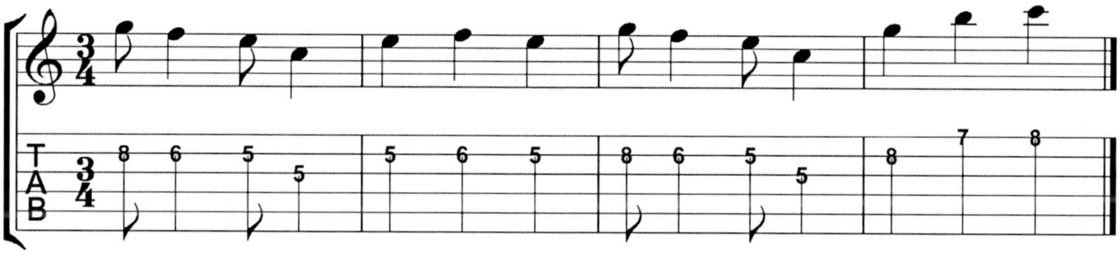

Example 2 from A major scale (CD track 15)

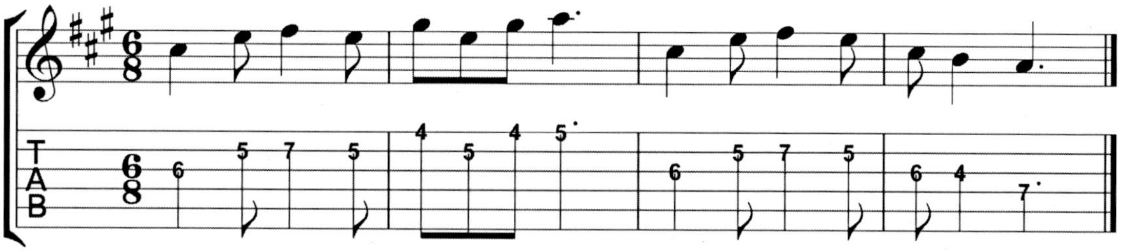

Test E – Recognising chord movements

The candidate should look away while the examiner plays a four bar chord sequence in the key of either C, G or D major. The first three chords will be either I IV V or I V IV. The final chord will be one of the minor chords in that key (IIm, IIIm or VIm). The examiner will then name the key, and the candidate should identify all of the chords in the sequence by naming them in the correct order.

Below are all of the chord sequences that may be played in this test. (Roman numerals are printed for reference only; answers should be given as chord names.) Some examples, in the key of C major, are provided on CD track 16.

Chord Sequence: I IV V IIm

Key: C major
Chords Played: C F G Dm

Key: G major
Chords Played: G C D Am

Key: D major
Chords Played: D G A Em

Chord Sequence: I V IV IIm

Key: C major
Chords Played: C G F Dm

Key: G major
Chords Played: G D C Am

Key: D major
Chords Played: D A G Em

Chord Sequence: I IV V IIIm

Key: C major
Chords Played: C F G Em

Key: G major
Chords Played: G C D Bm

Key: D major
Chords Played: D G A F♯m

Chord Sequence: I V IV IIIm

Key: C major
Chords Played: C G F Em

Key: G major
Chords Played: G D C Bm

Key: D major
Chords Played: D A G F♯m

Chord Sequence: I IV V VIm

Key: C major
Chords Played: C F G Am

Key: G major
Chords Played: G C D Em

Key: D major
Chords Played: D G A Bm

Chord Sequence: I V IV VIm

Key: C major
Chords Played: C G F Am

Key: G major
Chords Played: G D C Em

Key: D major
Chords Played: D A G Bm

RGT
Registry of Guitar Tutors

EXAMINATION ENTRY FORM
ACOUSTIC GUITAR
GRADE EIGHT

ONLINE ENTRY – AVAILABLE FOR UK CANDIDATES ONLY

For **UK candidates**, entries and payments can be made online at www.RegistryOfGuitarTutors.com, using the entry code below. You will be able to pay the entry fee by credit or debit card at a secure payment page on the website.

Your unique and confidential examination entry code is:

AH-2850-AQ

Keep this code *confidential*, as it can only be used once: if someone else uses it you will not be able to enter online and you will need to complete the form below and post it to the RGT office with a cheque for your entry fee.

If NOT entering online, please complete BOTH sides of this form and return to the address overleaf.

SESSION (Spring/Summer/Winter): ____________________ YEAR: ____________

Dates/times NOT available: ______________________________________

Note: Only name *specific* dates (and times on those dates) when it would be *absolutely impossible* for you to attend due to important prior commitments (such as pre-booked overseas travel) which cannot be cancelled. We will then endeavour to avoid scheduling an exam session in your area on those dates. In fairness to all other candidates in your area, only list dates on which it would be impossible for you to attend. An entry form that blocks out unreasonable periods may be returned. (Exams may be held on any day of the week including, but not exclusively, weekends. Exams may be held within or outside of the school term.)

Candidate Details: *Please write as clearly as possible using BLOCK CAPITALS*

Candidate Name (as to appear on certificate): ______________________________

Address: ____

____

______________________________ Postcode: ____________

Tel. No. (day): ____________________ (evening): ____________________

(mobile): ____________________ Email: ____________________________

Teacher Details *(if applicable)*

Teacher Name (as to appear on certificate): ______________________________

RGT Tutor Code (if applicable): ______________

Address: ____

____

______________________________ Postcode: ____________

Tel. No. (day): ____________________ (evening): ____________________

(mobile): ____________________ Email: ____________________________

RGT Acoustic Guitar Official Entry Form

The standard LCM entry form is NOT valid for Acoustic Guitar exam entries.
Entry to the examination is only possible via this original form.
Photocopies of this form will not be accepted under *any* circumstances.

- Completion of this entry form is an agreement to comply with the current syllabus requirements and conditions of entry published at www.RegistryOfGuitarTutors.com. Where candidates are entered for examinations by a teacher/parent/guardian that person hereby takes responsibility that the candidate is entered in accordance with the current syllabus requirements and conditions of entry.
- If you are being taught by an *RGT registered* tutor, please hand this completed form to your tutor and request him/her to administer the entry on your behalf.
- For candidates with special needs, a letter giving details should be attached.

Examination Fee: £__________________ Late Entry Fee (if applicable): £__________________

Total amount submitted: £________________

Cheques or postal orders should be made payable to Registry of Guitar Tutors.

Details of conditions of entry, entry deadlines and examination fees are obtainable from the RGT website: www.RegistryOfGuitarTutors.com

Once an entry has been accepted, entry fees cannot be refunded.

CANDIDATE INFORMATION (UK Candidates only)

In order to meet our obligations in monitoring the implementation of equal opportunities policies, UK candidates are required to supply the information requested below. *The information provided will in no way whatsoever influence the marks awarded during the examination.*

Date of birth: ________________ Age: ________ Gender – please circle: male / female

Ethnicity (please enter 2 digit code from chart below): ______ Signed: ____________________

ETHNIC ORIGIN CLASSIFICATIONS (If you prefer not to say, write '17' in the space above.)

White: **01 British** **02 Irish** **03 Other white background**

Mixed: **04 White & black Caribbean** **05 White & black African** **06 White & Asian** **07 Other mixed background**

Asian or Asian British: **08 Indian** **09 Pakistani** **10 Bangladeshi** **11 Other Asian background**

Black or Black British: **12 Caribbean** **13 African** **14 Other black background**

Chinese or Other Ethnic Group: **15 Chinese** **16 Other** **17 Prefer not to say**

I understand and accept the current syllabus regulations and conditions of entry for this examination as specified on the RGT website.

Signed by candidate (if aged 18 or over) ________________________ Date ____________

If candidate is under 18, this form should be signed by a parent/guardian/teacher (circle which applies):

Signed ____________________ Name __________________________ Date ____________

UK ENTRIES

See overleaf for details of how to enter online OR return this form to:
Registry of Guitar Tutors, Registry Mews, 11 to 13 Wilton Road, Bexhill-on-Sea, E. Sussex, TN40 1HY
Tel: 01424 22 22 22
(If you have submitted your entry and payment online you do not need to return this form.)

NON-UK ENTRIES

To locate the address within your country that entry forms should be sent to, and to view exam fees in your currency, visit the RGT website **www.RegistryOfGuitarTutors.com** and navigate to the 'RGT Worldwide' section.